LINCOLN AS IT WAS
Volume III

Compiled on behalf of
Lincolnshire Library Service
by
LAURENCE ELVIN, F.S.A., F.R.Hist.S., F.R.S.A.

Front cover : Lincoln Cathedral from Brayford, drawn by John O'Connor and engraved by
B. Lasbury. From The Stationers' Company's Almanac, 1878.

Published by Hendon Publishing Company Limited, Hendon Mill, Nelson, Lancashire
© *Lincolnshire County Library 1979*
Printed by Fretwell & Brian Ltd., Howden Hall, Silsden, Keighley, West Yorkshire

One of the finest and most rare early nineteenth century engravings of the city is this view from just below High Bridge, drawn by W. H. Bartlett for *Britton's Picturesque Antiquities of English Cities*, published by Longman & Co. of London on 11th May 1829. The tall and extensive building with arched entrance and two arched windows above, beyond the obelisk, was the Spread Eagle Hotel (converted to a store by F. W. Woolworth & Co. Ltd. in 1923) and beyond the Stonebow was the church of St. Peter-at-Arches, demolished in 1933 and rebuilt to serve the new parish of St. Giles. A small market was held in those days in the vicinity of the obelisk. Note the lower level of High Street on the extreme right.

Lincoln Minster, south view from the City Prison and Court House (later known as the Sessions House). A lithograph from the original water colour drawing by Frederick Mackenzie (1787–1854) in the collection of Richard Ellison of Sudbrooke Holme, published by W. & B. Brooke, Lincoln in 1853. On the hillside between the Old Palace and Lindum Road (cut in 1786 and originally named the New Road) were the Temple Gardens, a pleasure resort to which subscribers had a key, the public not normally being admitted except on special occasions. Their heyday was in the middle period of Queen Victoria's reign when fêtes, brass band contests, exhibitions and balloon ascents were the principal diversions. In 1863 the gardens closed down when the land was sold to J. M. Collingham the draper, who built a large house at the bottom corner fronting Lindum Road. This was demolished to make way for the splendid landscaping of the Usher Gallery which was opened in 1927.

(below) A train on the Manchester, Sheffield and Lincolnshire Railway is seen passing over the bridge spanning the Witham on its way to Grimsby, and on the river a steam packet is setting out on its journey to Boston.

These delightful engravings together with a number of others, published by Rock and Co., London, as an album of Lincoln views, show various aspects of the city between 1852–53. Then, as now, The Cornhill *(above)* was dominated by the handsome building with the classical front. This was the first Corn Exchange; designed by W. A. Nicholson it was opened in 1848. In the same year the market stalls were removed from High Street to The Cornhill. The tall building on the right was the Lincoln and Lincolnshire Fire Office and between it and the basket maker's shop on the corner, was the Dispensary (an institution for the medical relief of the poor) opened in 1826.

(right) Monks Abbey was a cell of St Mary's Abbey at York which belonged to the Benedictine Order. The community at Lincoln was a very small one with a prior and two or three monks; along with other religious houses it was dissolved by Henry VIII who appropriated the lands which were valued at £23. 6s. 3d. The grounds of the Abbey appear to have been very popular for games and picnics when this scene was engraved in 1852, for there was no Arboretum until twenty years later.

A woodcut of Bracebridge Church and Vicarage viewed from the Lincoln and Honington Railway in 1867 shows the rural character of the area which remained largely unspoilt until the building of the Manse estate by Lincoln Corporation about 1938. This meant the demolition of the fine old vicarage which the Revd. Charles Christopher Ellison had greatly enlarged in 1880. Vicar of Bracebridge and Rector of Boultham for many years, he was described as 'one of the most remarkable men of his generation'. A specialist in rose growing, his gardens which comprised some four acres planted with thousands of roses were the envy of the neighbourhood and attracted crowds of visitors when they were open to the public. A proficient angler and one of the finest shots in the county, he also found time in his very busy life as a devoted parish priest and social worker to become a leading expert in the art of ivory and metal turning for which he won many medals. The London and Honington Railway connecting Lincoln with Grantham and thence to London was opened on 15th April 1867. To commemorate the event a dinner was held in the spacious goods shed at Caythorpe. This line was closed in 1965 when access to London was made possible by a connecting curve from the Midland line at Newark.

One of the earliest photographs in the Local Collection at the Central Library is this view of the Norman house at the corner of Steep Hill and Christ's Hospital Terrace, mistakenly called the house of Aaron the Jew. Built circa 1170 this view of the building was taken shortly after the re-setting and restoration of the upstairs twin window in 1878. Bobby Lee, one of the characters of the day, who combined the business of tailor, carpet maker, general dealer and newsagent, was a familiar figure in the streets of Lincoln as a newspaper seller. He is seen standing at the door of his shop, the window of which appears to be crowded with a miscellany of goods. The business of H. H. Brummitt, carver, gilder, picture frame maker and glass dealer was well known in the city. He also compiled an *Illustrated guide through Lincoln*, an advertisement for which can be seen above the shop door.

One of Lincoln's foremost photographers of the last century was R. Slingsby who achieved international fame. The exact date of his establishment is not known, but he was at 2 Norman Street in 1867 later removing to 168 High Street. Here he remained in business until 1896 when Harrisons succeeded him, maintaining the very highest standards in portraiture and commercial photography until their closure in 1959. This advertisement taken from *Kelly's Directory of Lincolnshire* for 1889 tells us not only something about Slingsby's photographic art, but is a delightful example of advertising of the period showing the variety of type faces employed. Much of Slingsby's business was concerned with supplying carte-de-visites of his sitters (a photograph $2\frac{1}{2}'' \times 4''$ in size). His work can be identified by this attractive imprint on the back of each portrait. This subject taken in 1872 is the Rev. J. Mansel, Vicar of St. Mark's Church, Lincoln. The current interest in Victorian and Edwardian photography puts an ever increasing value on Grandma's photographic albums which were handsomely bound with brass clasps and strong pages with cut insets, to take these and the larger size cabinet photographs.

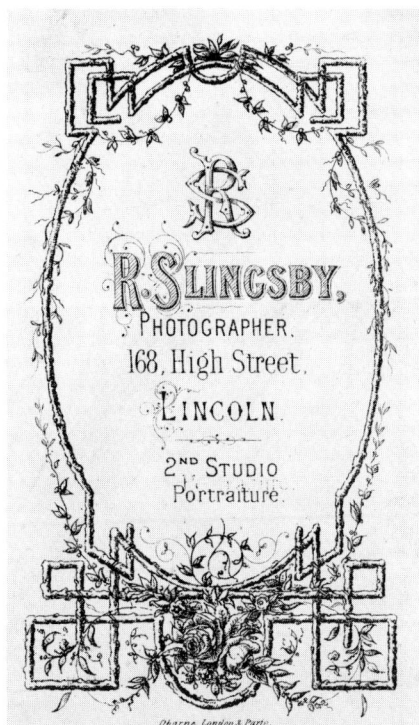

Yarborough Road, or Burton New Road as it was originally named, was made in stages. The final portion, some 1,300 yards in length and about 40 feet wide, extended from just below Long Leys Road to Burton Road at a point between the two groups of windmills which crowned the hill above the west common. This photograph shows the Mayor, Francis Jonathan Clarke (of Clarke's Blood Mixture fame and in his lifetime four times Mayor of Lincoln) at the ceremony of cutting the first sod on 2nd November 1880. The Mayoral procession headed by the band of Christ's Hospital Bluecoat School had marched to the site from the Guildhall. In the evening the Mayor gave a banquet at the Great Northern Hotel, thus concluding a memorable occasion in which he had played a part, for it was due to his untiring efforts that this project, mooted by Ald. R. Carline some thirty-six years previously, had been brought to fruition.

St. Benedict's Square with its medieval church and burial ground was a restful spot in the city centre at the time of this photograph in the late 1880s. This view from the south-west looks towards the Royal Hotel, 309 High Street established in 1867, the licensee of which was George Jennings. Seen on the extreme left of the north side of the square is the shop of John Davison Newbold and Son. The family in those days lived above the premises. Established in 1833 it was known as 'The People's Handy Shop'; shopkeepers and travellers were supplied 'on the lowest terms' and they also dealt in rags, bones, iron, bottles, horse hair, metals, hare and rabbit skins. When Marks & Spencer purchased the premises for extensions to their store, the scrap metal and waste part of the business was moved to Holmes Road.

The smaller room beyond the ballroom of the Assembly Rooms in Bailgate, built in 1744 has always been popular for dinners; on this occasion during January 1891 Lincoln Corporation was host to the Dean and Chapter. When these beautiful Georgian rooms were built candlelight was the method of illumination; this photograph shows the ornate gas chandeliers with their flare jets which were in use in the last century. The group at dinner includes E. Pratt, Mayor; the Dean, the Very Rev. W. J. F. Butler; the Archdeacon of Lincoln, the Ven. W. F. J. Kaye and Bishop Edward King standing by the fireplace. The Bishop became a legend in his lifetime for the saintliness of his character and his great capacity for friendship; everyone loved him and when he died in 1910 a local journalist wrote that Lincoln lay 'almost as under a pall'.

Bishop King was equally at home amongst working men and nothing gave him greater pleasure than mixing amongst them. Canon Scott Holland in *A Bundle of Memories* once wrote: 'It was a delicious experience to note the affection that followed him about. He draws out love as the sun draws out fragrance from the flowers.' Here is a picture which the Bishop always cherished, showing him amongst a group of men at the works of Clayton and Shuttleworth after addressing them in the mess-room during their breakfast half-hour on 6th May 1907.

These buildings at the north-west corner of Priorygate adjoined a large block of shops and cottages including The Dolphins Inn sited along the south side of Eastgate and effectively blocking the view of the Cathedral. The butcher's shop occupied by James W. Gambles was well situated for business in the Minster Yard area. Due to the munificence of Alfred Shuttleworth, the great industrialist, the whole property was demolished in March 1892.

The improvements to the Minster precincts instigated by Alfred Shuttleworth also included the demolition of two fine houses, No. 1 Minster Yard known as The Old College House immediately adjacent to the chapter house and No. 6 Priorygate, the subject of these photographs taken in 1891. In the seventeenth century these two houses formed one large residence which was known as 'College House'. This was not a place of education; the name applied to the whole cathedral body with its 'College' or 'Society' of Canons, Senior and Junior Vicars. The southern house, No. 1 Minster Yard (like its fellow, much altered particularly when the two houses were formed from the one) was picturesque but had no architectural features worthy of preservation. The northern residence however had the shell of a thirteenth century dining hall which was a very good example of the domestic architecture of the period. It had been erected by the Dean and Chapter as a refectory for the subordinate members of the body. After the whole area had been cleared, Minster Green was laid down and when the Tennyson Memorial Committee was looking for a site for the poet's statue, they decided to erect it where No. 6 Priorygate had once stood.

Removing materials during the demolition of the Priorygate property.

This dramatic photograph shows Rass Challis, lessee of the Theatre Royal, gazing at the ruins of the old building from the stage after the devastating fire on 26–27th November 1892 which marked the end of this historic little Theatre. In his hand is a bag of golden sovereigns, presumably the takings of the night before which had been kept in the safe. The fire had been burning through the night and was only discovered at 8.15 next morning; at the height of the blaze a tremendous explosion occurred which burst open the door facing the King's Arms and lifted off the roof which crashed into the pit. The explosion was caused by the ignition of a cylinder of oxygen used in producing lighting effects. Situated in the King's Arms yard, the Theatre was erected in 1806 on part of the consecrated ground of the demolished church of St. Lawrence. The building was typical of its time and could not have been very comfortable; the form seating in the pit will be noted as well as a few undamaged chairs in the dress circle. Pillars at regular intervals obstructed the view while the stage and dressing room area was small and inconvenient. Gas lighting had only been introduced just before the fire.

On the 14th January 1916 a special matinée of the pantomime 'Jack and the Beanstalk' was given at the Theatre Royal to an audience of wounded soldiers. Taken from the stage, this photograph shows the present building which was built immediately after the fire of 1892. Within the confines of restricted ground space, the architects Crewe and Sprague, of London were able to create a more roomy theatre, with a seating capacity of 840, a larger stage and no pillars to impede the view. Steel and concrete with the minimal use of wood was used in construction, as well as fireproof fibrous plaster. There was plush tip-up seating except in the gallery. The main entrance was in the King's Arms yard and this had to suffice until 1907 when a new entrance with foyer and upstairs lounge was built in Butchery Street (now named Clasketgate). The 'New Theatre' (which reverted to its old name of The Theatre Royal in 1907) was opened on the 18th December 1893. W. S. Penley's company from The Globe Theatre, London, was engaged to perform 'Charley's Aunt'. Prices of admission were fixed at £1. 11s. 6d. for private boxes; the dress circle was 8/-, stalls 2/-, pit 1/- and gallery 6d. These prices remained constant for many years!

Erected in 1813 by Lincoln Corporation to the design of
Ald. William Hayward (who was also responsible for the
Judges' Lodgings and Sessions House), Gowts Bridge with its
stone balustrading (still in existence), gas lamp, the cottages
nearby and the cobbled High Street with single line tram-
track, made an attractive picture for the photographer who
recorded the scene in 1894. Vernon Street was completed in
the following year, when Gilbert's Cottages were demolished
to make way for modern bay-windowed dwellings.

This attractive shop with its round-headed windows, situated just south of Swanpool Court, gives us some idea of the charm of Lincoln High Street in the middle of the last century when Cuthbert Wilks the chemist was in business there. This photograph taken in 1895 shows the bank occupying his old premises where he had traded since at least 1857. The bank of Peacock, Willson and Co. was founded in 1792 at Sleaford. Then known as Peacock, Handley and Kirton, after various changes of title it became Peacock, Willson and Co. in 1861. It was absorbed by Lloyds Bank in 1912.

By 1897 Peacock Willson's bank was occupying this fine new suite of premises on the site of Wilks' shop. The architect was William Watkins and he prepared some sixty to seventy full size drawings for Doulton's of Lambeth who carried out the work for the elaborate terra-cotta front. Inside, the main rooms were decorated with handsome fibrous plaster ceilings. The building is now occupied by the East Midlands Electricity Board.

Strawson's eating house was a very popular establishment in the city centre from the early 1870s until about 1920 when its curious hotch-potch building was pulled down, the northern portion making way for the shop of E. R. Dixon the chemist. Its upstairs rooms must have been rather airless with their small windows, but the Coffee Tavern as it was known, provided excellent meals at low prices. Hot dinners were only 6d, 9d and 1/- in the 1890s when this photograph was taken. R. Wingad the tobacconist, whose shop was at the corner of Swanpool Court, had been next door neighbour to Richard Adam Strawson since he commenced business. The fine display of walking sticks in the window, will be noticed. This busy little shop, which in early years included hairdressing, and the sale of perfume, continued under the name of G. R. Wingad & Sons until about 1967.

Lincoln postmen, a photograph taken about 1897 near the old sorting office in High Street just below the Midland (now St. Mark's) railway station.

On Monday evening 12th January 1891 in the small room of the Drill Hall, John Sambrook gave an inaugural lecture in connection with the opening of his private school at 19 Broadgate. His subject was: 'On Memory' and he announced that children attending his school would enjoy the advantages of his system in their training and studies. Two years previously he had written *Sambrook's phonographic system of mnemonics; Summary of class tuition* which was published by Akrill, Ruddock & Keyworth. In 1892 he was advertising: 'Sambrook's School of Memory, the best and cheapest school in England; languages, mathematics, book-keeping etc., 19 Broadgate, Lincoln, branch school above hill.' A further book, *Education without injury or how to strengthen memory; Sambrook's international assimilative system* was published in 1896. This rather unusual schoolmaster and lecturer apparently was successful with his school, for this photograph taken in the late 1890s shows twenty-three pupils of various ages and two assistant teachers. At this time there were about twenty private schools in the city. The school closed between 1903–4.

Laying a gas main in Baggeholme Road in the late 1890s. On the left is St. Swithin's C. of E. School and in the distance is the conduit which once stood at the junction of Baggeholme Road and Croft Street.

In the second half of Queen Victoria's reign there were several mineral water manufacturers in the city; for example in 1891 there were four businesses operating, now there are none. Bottles bearing such names as Arnold & Co., Bayne, Claxton, Giles and Taylor, Goulson, Martin Ltd., Parke and White and others are highly prized by collectors today. Kenneth Bayne established a business at 45 Broadgate in the early 1860s; by 1885 Eliza Bayne was proprietor and five years later the Drill Hall was built on the north side of her premises on land which hitherto had been occupied by Henry Newsum's timber manufactory. On the extreme left of this photograph of Broadgate taken soon after the Drill Hall was opened in 1890, is the Bayne residence which faced south on to a cobbled yard, the business being carried on in surrounding buildings. Louis Draper took over the Bayne concern in the late 1890s but his connection with it was only a short one, for Parke and White (est. 1840) had purchased it by 1899 and traded under their name from then onwards. Extensions to the premises fronting Broadgate completely obscured the house which became the manager's residence. The firm of Parke, White, Arnold and Co. traded at 45 Broadgate until their closure in 1961, the property then being purchased by the City Council for an extension to the Library and Museum.

This fine locomotive with its four great driving wheels was a 4–4–0 No. 561 built by Beyer, Peacock and Co. for the Manchester, Sheffield and Lincolnshire Railway in 1887. Engines of this type passed regularly through Lincoln in the latter years of Queen Victoria's reign. A number of companies amalgamated to form The Manchester, Sheffield and Lincolnshire Railway on 1st January 1847 and after some delay the Lincoln section was opened for traffic in 1850. The line from New Holland, Grimsby and Market Rasen entered the city over the level crossing into the Midland Station (now St. Mark's) where it had an end-on junction with the Midland line. The gate-house which is still in use is a relic of those early days. There was also a single line connection with the Great Northern Station at the Durham Ox Junction. In 1897 the M.S.L.R. was renamed The Great Central Railway.

Sincil Street has always been a picturesque and busy shopping centre in the heart of the city, with the covered New Market, the Corn Exchange and fruit market below as well as the semi-open market for fish, fruit, flowers and clothing adjoining the street. This photograph taken in 1899 shows the original New Market Hotel opened in 1856 and beyond is Elton Scott's yard, once known as the bone yard, being part of Doughty, Son and Richardson's Fertiliser Works. At that time rats were so numerous that dog owners were invited to spend days killing off the vermin! Elton Scott was an auctioneer and used the yard for sales for a number of years. Later on, Smith and Warren, amusement caterers housed their steam roundabout, swings and stalls in the yard during the winter months when not on tour and did a good business on Saturday nights well into the present century. The outside walls of the building were covered with large and colourful posters by the Lincoln Billposting Co. whose bill-stickers could be seen each week deftly arranging a new poster on many layers of old ones! The site is now occupied by the Central Market (opened in 1938) and the adjoining car park.

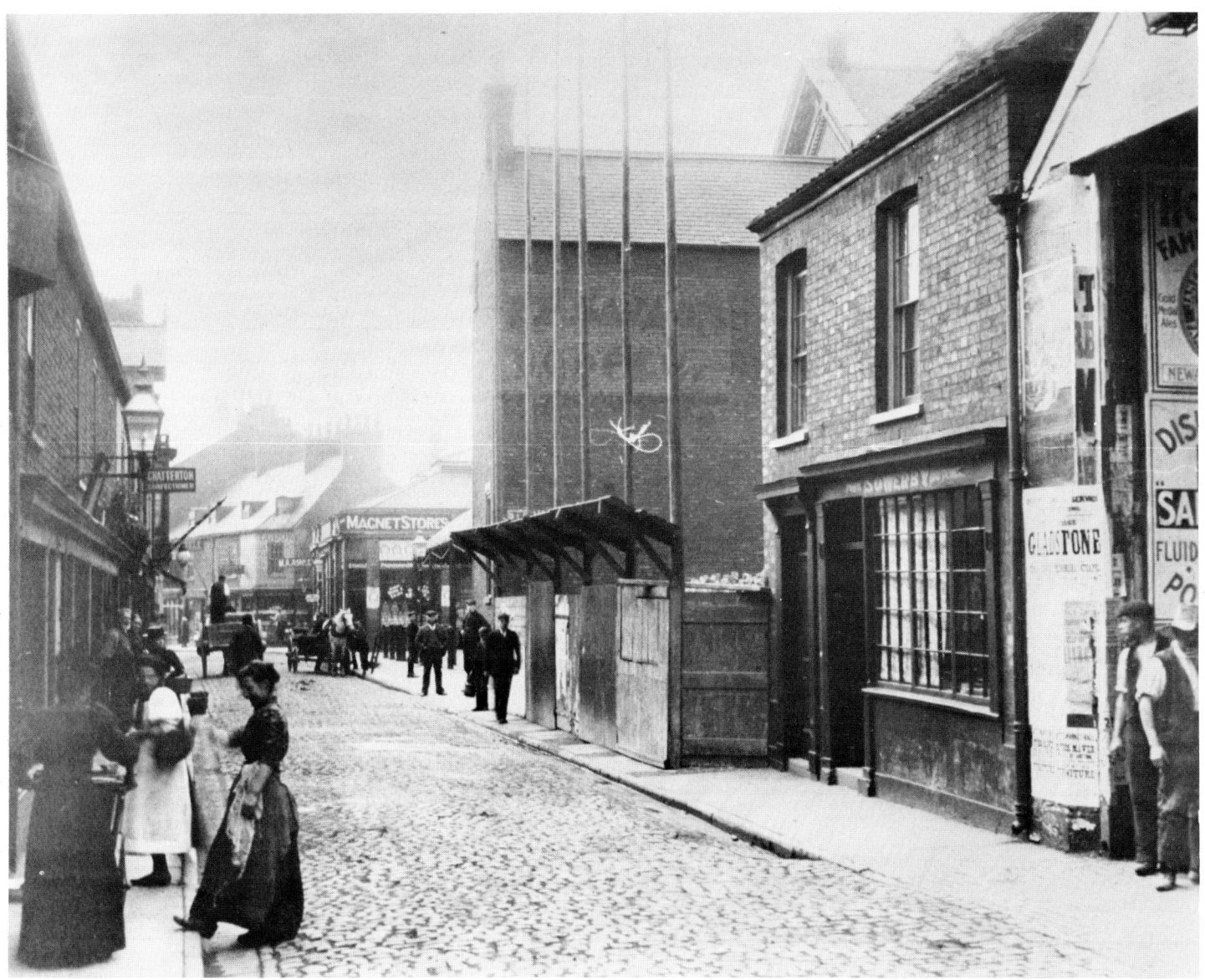

A second photograph taken in 1899 of Sincil Street looking south shows a number of well known businesses; on the west side, the old established pork butcher's shop of George Sowerby (now on the opposite side of the road), the Magnet grocery store and in the distance, T. Cook's the chemist and M. A. Ashley's pram, sewing machine and toy emporium. As well as a veritable rabbit-warren of courts and alleyways housing a large number of people in tiny cottages on the east side of the street, a wide variety of shop-keeping was carried on. The old established business of Chatterton & Son, noted for pork pies and potted meat, is seen on the left of the picture.

To enter the Lord Nelson Inn previous to road alterations in High Street carried out in 1907, one had to cross a bridge which spanned the steps down to Waterside North. The inn dated from 1794; the obelisk was erected in 1762 on the site of a former wayside chapel dedicated to St. Thomas à Becket of Canterbury. At the back of the obelisk was a gent's urinal with handsomely decorated cast iron screens of the Victorian period. The fish, game and poultry business of William Cooper had been established almost a hundred years; he claimed to supply leading county families, the Cathedral dignitaries and 'all the epicurean section of the community'. The fine display of game and poultry together with many varieties of fish, evidently was a source of great interest to the young man and elderly gentleman in the top hat. The sign, Jaeger Clothing was affixed to the shop of C. J. Fox & Co., Tailors and Outfitters.

The shop of Clifford Thomas, bookseller, stationer and printer on the south-west corner of High Street and St. Benedict's Square presented a striking sight, its windows crowded with goods when this photograph was taken in 1900. The business had traded here since circa 1857 when it was owned by Edward Ralph Cousans; later it became Cousans and Gale and the latter partner became sole owner until Thomas succeeded him. The Echo and Gazette office in St. Benedict's Square had partial connections with this old established firm. E. R. Cousans bought the *Lincoln Gazette* from J. E. Brogden in 1870. It appeared weekly on a Saturday and was eventually taken over by *The Lincolnshire Echo* (founded in 1893) which firm continued to publish it until some time in the 1920s.

As industry expanded in the city, so did banking and in 1903 when this photograph was taken, the Capital and Counties Bank (now Lloyds) had just opened their fine new suite of premises on the site of Clifford Thomas's shop at the corner of High Street and St. Benedict's Square. Designed in the Georgian Baroque style with cupola (since removed), the architects were William Mortimer and Son of Lincoln.

After the construction of Corporation Street between 1896–97 the first section of a large block of property was built which eventually extended from the High Street corner to Hungate. This photograph of Dixon and Parker's clothiers and outfitters shop was taken in 1901. Their window displays were typical of the overcrowding of those days while their bills advertising 'Gent's Business Suits 45/- to measure, a speciality' foreshadowed the supermarket frontages of today. Above the shop, Erdmann Voss, with his London West End Hairdressing Saloon and Salon Modes, Millinery, were high class establishments with a good clientele.

This photograph taken from the beginning of West Parade shows the Monson Arms Tap and the group of shops which were built as the second stage of the Corporation Street property on its north side, joining up with the Lincoln Cycle Company and Dixon and Parker's to form an extensive suite of premises with spacious accommodation above. On the top floor and running the full length of the building was a dining hall belonging to the Monson Arms, with seating accommodation for nearly 200 people. This hotel which stood just above Dixon & Parker's in High Street, was established in 1787 when it was then known as The Black Bull Inn. Demolished in 1962 it gave its name to a new hotel on Skellingthorpe Road, Swanpool.

Shepherd's Skin Yard, a country scene at the east end of Ashton's Court, High Street, St. Peter-at-Gowt's in 1901. The land was already earmarked for the completion of Abbot, Prior and Nelthorpe Streets which had been commenced some four years previously. Samuel Shepherd, who had established his fellmonger's business here circa 1885 (he prepared skins for the tanner) removed to Newark Road where he continued until about 1907.

On the south side of Ashton's Court with 393 High Street in between and but a stone's throw from St. Peter-at-Gowt's Church, was Linton Place, a tightly packed community of nine cottages, those on the west side being the subject of this photograph taken in 1901. The presence of the women enjoying a gossip at the cottage door and the old man further along with a black cat in the yard, help to create atmosphere to a scene which otherwise would be very drab.

A photograph of West's stores at 115c and 115d High Street in 1901. The business was founded by W. E. West as a barber's shop on Canwick Road in 1887. He was quick to see the future of the cycle and started dealing there, being one of the first in the county to do so. He moved to larger premises in High Street in 1900 where trade was considerably expanded, for as the internal combustion engine developed, motor cycles and the odd car were sold. There was also a department for the sale and repair of phonographs, while the barber's shop continued together with a wholesale and retail tobacco trade. In common with many other business people in those days, Mr. and Mrs. West and their family lived above the shop. The large stone house known as John O'Gaunt's House (though having no historic association with John O'Gaunt) on the right of the photograph, was occupied at this time by Dr. Walter Jagger (of Daman and Jagger, Surgeons). C. B. Brimlow's draper's shop adjoining West's on the south side not long afterwards became the Public Benefit Boot Co. The whole block eventually was taken over by West's who demolished John O'Gaunt's House to make way for their garage and showrooms.

The restoration of the sixteenth century property on High Bridge during 1901 was an extensive undertaking and to Lincoln Corporation, the owners, belongs the credit of being the first to carry out major restoration of a half-timbered building in the city. They engaged William Watkins, architect and Halkes Bros., builders, both of Lincoln, to carry out the work. George Hood's boot and shoe shop at 211–212 High Street, had been there since about 1870; his advertising was always designed to catch the eye such as: 'Stylish shoes for dainty feet, pretty shoes for little feet, easy boots for tender feet, wide boots for broad feet!' The Lincoln Coffee Palace was a popular eating house with extensive dining rooms, then under the management of Mrs. Glass, who also was adept at advertising, drawing attention to the many amenities as follows: 'Breakfasts, dinners and teas daily, special accommodation for private dinner and other parties at shortest notice. Chops and steaks at any hour. Cloak room accommodation for ladies and lavatories free. London, provincial and illustrated papers. Hot joints daily, 12.00–3.00 and special market dinners on Tuesdays and Fridays.' R. W. Stokes took over the Coffee Palace about 1919 and renamed it The Arcadia Cafe. The site is now part of Marks and Spencer's frontage. Clifford Thomas at 206 High Street, had transferred his business there in 1900 when his former premises at the corner of St. Benedict's Square were demolished for the new Capital and Counties Bank.

(opposite) Five years after the Diamond Jubilee of Queen Victoria in 1897 Lincoln had another joyful occasion to celebrate – the Coronation of King Edward VII on 9th August 1902. Despite wet weather which had interfered with the work of street decorating, the city centre presented a gay appearance on the day. The Stonebow, decorated with ferns, plants and flowers was lit by electric fairy lights for the first time; electricity had only been generated in the city since 1899 and Mr. Stanley Clegg, the Electrical Engineer had the task of organising the Stonebow lighting. Three years before, for the Diamond Jubilee event, long burning candles in coloured jars had been used! The main streets were ablaze at night with various forms of lighting on public and private buildings and in the Sessions House grounds hung with Chinese lanterns and coloured lights, music was provided by the Malleable Iron Works Band. The pièce de resistance however was a beacon of light with 40,000 candle power, placed on top of the central tower of the Cathedral which could be seen for miles around.

(below) For some years after the 1914–18 war, Cousans, Sons & Co. also ran the 'Brayford Garage' where they had a modern plant of machine tools, pits and lifter tackle enabling them to carry out all kinds of repairs including oxy-acetylene welding, brazing, forging and the making of spare parts. Here too, they converted Crossley ex army tenders into buses. This photograph shows their haulage and furniture removing van outside their premises. It was in fact an open dray with a detachable van and thus was a forerunner of the modern container lorry. It was too tall to go through the low arch into the firm's yard so the crane which then stood on the wharf side nearby was used to detach the van section from the lorry!

Photographed in 1902 the interior of the factory of Cousans, Sons and Co., organ builders, at the corner of Cathedral Street and Lindum Road, was typical of a number of small craft businesses which flourished years ago before the advent of mass production. The firm was founded in 1877 by J. R. Cousans in Croft Street; his son Reginald Arthur is standing behind the bicycle at the back of the workshop. He was a skilled engineer as well as an organ builder of great ability. During the First World War at extensive premises between Newland and Brayford, the firm was engaged in the manufacture of munitions. The Cathedral Street building was vacated during the war and after hostilities ceased, organ building was carried on in much more spacious premises at 20a Newland and Brayford Wharf until their demolition in 1975.

This splendid photograph of an early Wolseley car takes us back to the Edwardian era of gracious living, with the elegant fashions of the ladies and a determination on the part of those who could afford it to enjoy themselves. This occasion was probably a rally of the Lincolnshire Automobile Club held in the castle grounds in 1902. The Keep is seen in the background and on the left, the old court buildings and prison.

The Unitarian Chapel at the corner of High Street and Monson Street built in 1725 is the second oldest nonconformist building in the city, the first being the Friends' Meeting House in Park Street, dating from 1689. The chapel with its red brick walls, was a simply designed meeting house as shown in this photograph taken in 1902 before a comprehensive restoration and re-ordering of the building was commenced. The exterior took on the look we know today, with cement rendered walls, a more elaborate front with ornamented pediment and porch together with stained glass windows. The interior fittings were swept away in favour of oak pews, altar and pulpit in almost Anglican style. The finely moulded ceiling with its centre rose and two sturdy wood pillars supporting the roof (tradition says they are former ship's masts) are reminders of earlier days. The chapel has an atmosphere all its own and deserves to be better known.

St. Mary's Street after widening in the early 1900s had a spacious appearance and it must have rejoiced the hearts of the City Fathers who felt that it would be more than adequate to cope with traffic for many years ahead. They could not possibly have foreseen the congestion caused by the ever growing number of cars and lorries in a street which has become the main artery for traffic from all directions. The cab rank as now was on the north side of St. Mary-le-Wigford's Church; the cabbies' shelter can be seen in the station yard. Above the well known shop of Hodson and White, saddlers, Lance Holtby had a photographic studio for a number of years. He was also a painter in water colours and became well known for his Lincoln scenes which were exhibited at the Lincolnshire Artists' Society Exhibitions. The Albion Hotel, a tall and spacious building erected in 1867, also housed on its west side The Lincoln Club.

The smoke room of the Albion Hotel created by the Lincoln architect William Watkins in the style of a Moorish palace, was a source of wonder to all who visited the hotel for the first time. Some idea of its splendour can be seen from the photograph; it was octagonal in shape with a dome-like ceiling. The colour scheme was red and gold while the seating was 'quite unique in character being divided by raised arms into what was virtually a row of comfortable arm chairs, a sunk recess being contrived in each arm in which the occupant of the seat might place his glass, while there was also accommodation for ash tray and matches'. There was a quaint little bar partly hidden by curtains, Japanese in design, while the bar fittings, tables and chairs were of teak. The lighting was most ingenious, 'giving here an appearance of a glorious summer sunset, there the idea of the soft rays of a clear, full moon scintillating on the decorations'. The room had the seductive atmosphere of the Orient and showed the versatility of its designer. Alas, it was demolished about 1960 and replaced by a conventional lounge bar.

The 'Lincoln Elk' cycles and motor cycles once were famous throughout the world and are now much sought after as collectors' pieces. J. Kirby began making cycles at his premises in Broadgate in 1891 and in the autumn of 1902 the first motor cycle bearing the name the 'Lincoln Elk' was introduced to the public. It was an immediate success and was noted for its simplicity, reliability and cheapness. As the years went by, improvements were made to keep up with the times; everything with the exception of tyres, magneto and carburettor was manufactured at the Broadgate premises and each machine was tested 'on the road and on the trying hills around Lincoln' to quote the catalogue of 1920. At this time, prices ranged from a few shillings under sixty pounds for the 2¾ h.p. lightweight model to the 6 h.p. model at £126 10s. 0d. This photograph of the showrooms and manufactory at Nos. 4–5 Broadgate (the Post Office Telephone Exchange now occupies the site), was taken in the early 1900s, by which time the firm was known as Kirby and Edwards. The 1909 directory of Lincoln names J. Kirby as the sole proprietor and he appears to have ceased trading sometime in the 1920s.

The Cattle Market, Lincoln.

A busy scene at the cattle market, Monks Road in the early 1900s. The market closed in 1968 and the selling of sheep and cattle is no longer carried on in the city. The land is now occupied by the College of Technology.

After the widening of St. Mark's Lane, this photograph was taken in 1907. Harrison's Malleable Iron Works on the left was part of the city scene from its establishment in 1874 until the premises were demolished in 1928 to make way for the City Transport garage. This casting business was founded by three enterprising Lincoln businessmen: Mr. F. H. Harrison, J.P., Mr. J. H. Teague and Mr. J. Birch. It amalgamated with the Hykeham Foundry Company in 1904 and the business still continues there under the title of Leys Malleable Castings Co. Ltd. The entrance to the Great Central Railway goods yard and cattle depot is seen on the extreme right of the photograph. The attractively designed gas lamp was typical of those used to light Lincoln streets at this time.

An unusual view of St. Mark's Church from the south-west, photographed in the early 1900s, shows part of the Great Central Railway goods yard. The church, built to the design of William Watkins and consecrated on 25th July 1872 was demolished in 1972.

Lincoln races were first held as long ago as 1597 and King James I saw 'a great horse race' at Lincoln on 3rd April 1617. By 1669 the sport had become so popular that a number of persons of 'honour and quality applied for horse races to be set up annually for ever'. Land eventually was purchased on Lincoln Heath on a site now occupied by the R.A.F. airfield at Waddington; annual racing commenced there in 1680 and continued until 1773 when it was decided to move to the present West Common. From then onwards racing at Lincoln really began to develop, five days being given over to the event which then took place after harvesting; later this was reduced to three days and the Lincoln meeting became a firm fixture immediately following the Doncaster races. The event with the famous race, The Lincolnshire Handicap first run in 1849 was one of the most notable of its kind in the country and in its heyday attracted enormous crowds. This photograph was taken in 1905 by R. Marris of Steep Hill. During the 1950s support began to fade and the Lincoln Corporation Race Committee, who since 1939 had been responsible for the meeting, reluctantly decided to cease racing on the Carholme after March 1964.

(opposite) Samuel Patton seen at the door of his shop at 198 High Street in the early 1900s, came from Kensington to Lincoln in 1879 to bake for John Seely of 188 High Street, at a wage of 30/- per week. Here, in addition to his normal daily duties, he had to carry out what was known as 'Public Baking' on a Sunday morning. This meant getting the ovens hot to receive the joint and pudding of families who left them on their way to church for collection afterwards – all ready for consumption on arrival at home! It meant a day of rest for the privileged but a busy morning for a hard worked baker. Patton set up on his own as a pastrycook and confectioner at 335 High Street circa 1885 and later took the shop at 198 with bakery behind, formerly occupied by Henry Poppleton, confectioner. Upstairs was a small café which did good business at weekends. The site is now part of British Home Stores. Postcards such as these were useful advertising media, today they are prized collectors' items.

The unveiling of the Tennyson statue by Lady Brownlow on Minster Green on the 15th July 1905 in the presence of Hallam, Lord Tennyson; Bishop King; The Mayor, (Ald. Hugh Wyatt) and a distinguished gathering from the city and county. The Cathedral choir was present and under the direction of Dr. G. J. Bennett, Organist and Master of The Choristers, sang Tennyson's *Crossing the bar* to the setting of Sir Frederick Bridge. The Poet Laureate's old friend, G. F. Watts, R.A., O.M., completed the bronze statue when he was eighty-six years of age; unfortunately he did not live to see its erection on Minster Green. Clad in an Inverness cloak, deep in thought over a simple flower in his hand, the poet is accompanied by his beloved dog Karenina – a Siberian wolfhound. The base of the statue some 9 ft. 6 ins. high is of Polyphant marble; the design was the gift of Mr. C. Turnor of Panton Hall, Wragby.

In contrast to the present day, upper High Street in the early 1900s was an important and busy shopping centre. This photograph dated 1906 shows much activity amongst the many and varied businesses in the area. The focal point of the picture is the shop of Boots Cash Chemists. At that time in their *Guide to Lincoln* published in 1899 they said: 'The situation of this branch for business is the finest imaginable; it is an ideal corner and Messrs. Boots have not been slow to make the most of it . . . Crowds may daily be seen round the windows, and no wonder, for Messrs. Boots, apart from the various classes of goods – many necessary and others desirable – they sell, have a way of their own of displaying their merchandise which is really magnetic.' It is interesting to recall that the original shop of Boots the Chemists in High Street near the Midland Station (St. Mark's), was opened on 25th October 1884 and Lincoln was one of the first towns to have a branch of the rapidly expanding Nottingham business.

Part of Henry Kirke White's Lindum Restaurant above the shop of Clipsham and Payne, family grocers, 188 High Street at the corner of Brayford Street. The long dining room could accommodate 300 persons and was a popular venue for parties, whist drives, dances and other social occasions. Smaller rooms were full to capacity on Fridays and Saturdays, when in the early 1900s one could enjoy a three course lunch for only 2/-. Bent-wood chairs were hardly an inducement to linger over a meal but there was a full staff of waitresses to give speedy service. The flowers on each table made the room welcoming; the ladies in the corner enjoying a meal and a chat no doubt were delighted to be included in this photograph taken about 1907.

This is the scene in Lincoln High Street which greeted King Edward VII and his companions, the Grand Duke of Hesse and Prince Albert of Greece on the 26th June 1907 as they drove from the Great Northern Railway Station to the West Common on the occasion of the Royal Show. The arch which spanned the road from Peacock Willson's bank on the west side and the Queen Hotel on the east, had a model of a portable Ruston engine flanked on either side by ploughs, the whole display together with that in Guildhall Street, portraying the industries of the city.

Armed militia operating the level crossings of the Great Northern Railway during the railway strike in August 1911.

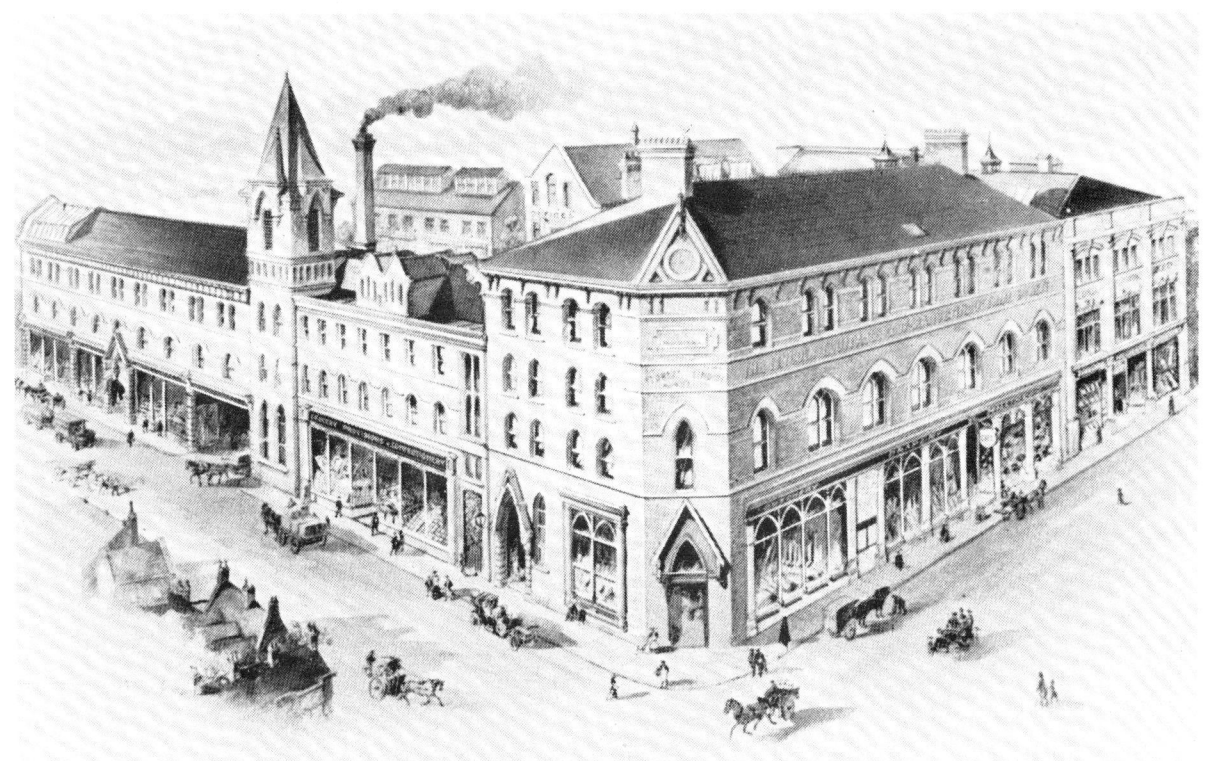

The extensive premises of the Lincoln Co-operative Society in Silver Street and Free School Lane as they appeared in 1911. When the Society was little more than ten years old (this was in May 1872) they decided to buy the site and erect 'a very substantial and beautiful building, Gothic in style', three storeys high. On the 1st January 1874 it was opened with a tea party and a public meeting in the large hall on the top floor, which could accommodate 1000 to 1200 people. A three storey block in Free School Lane for the sale of furniture, crockery, tailoring, boots and shoes, together with a library and reading rooms was opened on 2nd November 1889 and further extensions were completed in 1910. Then in 1933 the former General Dispensary premises adjoining the Silver Street building were purchased with a view to future development. All but the southern portion of the old block in Free School Lane was demolished to make way for a new store built between 1964–65.

The Women's Guild has played an active part in the affairs of the Lincoln Co-operative Society ever since November 1892 when the first Guild was started. There was a rapid response to the invitation for members and before very long they had raised the sum of £7 7s. 5d. for gymnasium fittings to be used by a class of young girls. A Mrs. Hodgett who was one of the first members, was President of the National Guild Congress at Blackpool in 1901 and two years later she presided at a similar meeting held at Lincoln. This photograph shows a gathering of the Central branch (location unknown) together with husbands, children and friends in the early 1900s.

Free School Lane was an interesting hotch-potch of buildings when this photograph was taken in 1912. On the west side beyond the Co-operative Society building was a group of houses, the last one being occupied by the Revd. Bernard Hancock, Vicar of St. Swithin's Church. Returning, on the other side was the Free School Lane Council School, the headmistress of which was Miss Clarice E. Hughes. Then came the Co-operative Society's pork butcher's shop followed by the residence of Mr. G. Musgrave with his tool merchant's business next door. Above the Co-op greengrocer's shop at the corner of Silver Street was the office of C. W. Page, accountant and organist at Wesley Chapel, Clasketgate until his death in 1912.

Ruston and Proctor played a tremendous part in the manufacture of munitions during the First World War. Man power was one of the greatest difficulties encountered by the management and women were brought in, not only for light tasks but for the turning of shells and even the forging of ingots. The peak of their production was in 1917 when this photograph of one of the immense bays of the Boultham works was taken. A woman worker is seen on the extreme right.

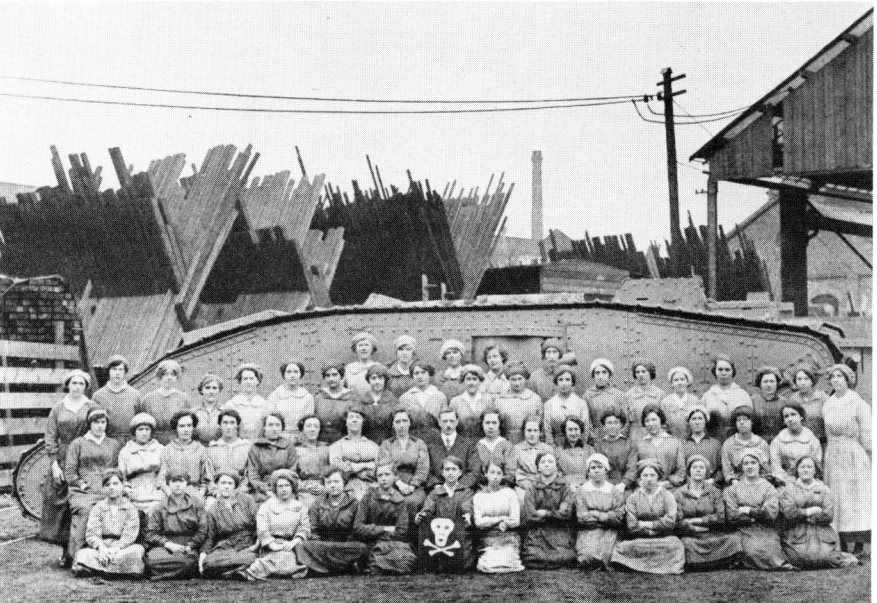

There has been a certain amount of controversy as to who actually did invent the tank in the First World War, but the truth of the matter can be summed up in the statement made by the Royal Commission on Awards to Inventors in October 1919 which reads as follows: 'Sir William Tritton and Major Wilson. It is to these two claimants that we attribute the credit of designing and producing in a concrete practical shape, the novel and efficient engine of warfare known as the tank.' Major W. G. Wilson, a motor and civil engineer of considerable experience who had been working under the Landships Committee of the Government was sent to Lincoln to co-operate with Mr. W. A. Tritton, managing director of William Foster and Co. They pooled their ideas and as a result, the first machine named 'Little Willie' was produced in 1915. An improved version known as the 'Mother type' went into action on the Somme in 1916 and was such an outstanding success that Fosters were urged by the Government to proceed with their construction with all speed. Other models that followed were 'The Whippet' and 'The Hornet'. Mr. Tritton received a knighthood on 13th February 1917 as a tribute to the predominant role he had taken in the evolution of the tank. This photograph shows General Sir William Robertson (later Field Marshal) at Foster's Wellington Foundry, New Boultham on 2nd March 1918 to inspect tank production. On the right of the photograph are Sir William and Lady Tritton.

Some of the female employees who helped to make the tank at Foster's Wellington Foundry.

The Globe Inn, Waterside South was one of a number which served the needs of the workers from Ruston's, Clayton and Shuttleworth's, Rainforth's, Cooke's Plough Works and others in the densely populated area of Waterside and Stamp End. The building shown here, photographed sometime during the 1920s replaced an earlier inn opened in 1811. The first licensee, Mr. Thomas Miller was a former groom to Lord Monson; when he embarked on his new career he advertised good stabling and signified his intention of running a farrier's business as well. He had just begun to make a name for himself when three years later on 30th January 1814 he suffered a fatal accident on a horse in the parish of Potter Hanworth.

This delightful example of a bill-head of the period, made out to Richard Carline in the year 1840, belonged to George Smith, maltster, whose premises were just west of the original Globe Inn at 28 Waterside South. The Old Crown Brewery later occupied the site, now not a vestige remains of the tightly packed property which existed for so many years on the south bank of the river.

One of Lincoln's first buses with solid tyres and slatted wooden seats – a far cry from the comfort of today. It was one of a batch of eleven vehicles which commenced running in 1920. With a Dennis chassis and engine, they had single decker bodies built by Frank Allen Ltd. of Brigg. The passengers seen in this photograph were employees with their wives, children and friends on a departmental outing.

Ever since picture postcards have been on sale, views of High Street have been second only in popularity to the Cathedral. This photograph was taken in 1928, a year before the trams disappeared from the Lincoln street scene. The Black Bull Hotel seen on the left was first licensed in 1794 and in those days was residential as well as a beer house. In the days of the carrier's cart it was one of a number of hotels where the carriers could park their carts and stable their horses on reaching the city from the county. From 1905–37 the licensee was Bill Spencer who was also a horse dealer, cabman, and in his early days held the contract for driving the post office mails. In later years the Black Bull had the distinction of being the first public house in the city to have television in its public rooms. Until its closure in 1961 it was a favourite drinking place for farmers and countrymen at weekends. The site is now occupied by British Home Stores.

After dealing with the worst of Lincoln's slums, in 1933 the City Council adopted a five year plan involving the demolition of a further 666 houses. The city was divided into clearance areas and photographs were taken of examples of sub-standard property in each. The houses were far from picturesque although these cottages, numbers 3–9 St. Rumbold Street had more character than most, the whole having the air of a group of country cottages.

Unity Street, off Friars Lane consisted of some fifteen dwellings, this photograph showing the backs of numbers 1–7. The woman filling her kettle from the communal tap in the yard and the poorly clad child (this was in the depression of the 1930s) add human interest to an otherwise dismal scene. This property and that in St. Rumbold Street was demolished between 1937–39.